CW00518024

Swimming in the soup [...] us saturated with the [...] led in submission to [...] obedience to any outside authority—especially God. But doing so is disastrous. Following 'my truth' rather than 'God's Truth' undermines our flourishing journey through life and has grave consequences regarding where we will spend eternity. This little book on apologetics from my friend Stephen Nichols is packed full of big, life-altering truths that will equip you to both find and give answers to the hard questions of faith and life.

Walt Mueller
President of the Center for Parent/Youth Understanding
Author of *A Student's Guide to Navigating Culture*

At last! An apologetics book that is practical rather than academic, biblical rather than philosophical, entertaining rather than boring, short rather than long, and, most importantly, Christ-centered rather than Christless. This engaging and enjoyable book will not only defend your faith but help you defend and share the faith with others.

David Murray
(Senior Pastor, First Byron CRC. Author of The StoryChanger, Jesus on Every Page, and other books)

If I needed an introduction to apologetics, and I do, this masterful primer by Stephen Nichols would be the one I'd choose. Apologetics can easily get into the weeds. The complexity of competing worldviews and the intricate nuances of various philosophies can easily lead into arguments that few can understand. But every Christian needs to defend what he or she believes about God, about Jesus. And every Christian needs to know how best to do it. And here, in this short primer, Nichols has given you a gem. It might even change your life. So be prepared to be changed, challenged, convicted, and encouraged.

Derek W. H. Thomas
Senior Minister, First Presbyterian Church, Columbia SC
Teaching Fellow, Ligonier Ministries
Chancellor's Professor, Reformed Theological Seminary

TRACK
DOCTRINE

A STUDENT'S GUIDE TO
APOLOGETICS

STEPHEN J.
NICHOLS

SERIES EDITED BY
JOHN PERRITT

CHRISTIAN
FOCUS

tjm

Scripture quotations are from *The Holy Bible, English Standard Version*, copyright © 2001 by Crossway Bibles, a publishing ministry of Good News Publishers. Used by permission. All rights reserved. ESV Text Edition: 2011.

Copyright © Stephen J. Nichols 2023

paperback ISBN 978-1-5271-0967-4

ebook ISBN 978-1-5271-0996-4

10 9 8 7 6 5 4 3 2 1

First published in 2023
by
Christian Focus Publications Ltd,
Geanies House, Fearn, Ross-shire,
IV20 1TW, Great Britain
www.christianfocus.com

with

Reformed Youth Ministries,
1445 Rio Road East
Suite 201D
Charlottesville,
Virginia, 22911

Cover by MOOSE77

Printed by Bell & Bain, Glasgow

CONTENTS

Series Introduction

Christianity is a religion of words, because our God is a God of words. He created through words, calls Himself the Living Word, and wrote a book (filled with words) to communicate to His children. In light of this, pastors and parents should take great efforts to train the next generation to be readers. *Track* is a series designed to do exactly that.

Written for students, the *Track* series addresses a host of topics in three primary areas: Doctrine, Culture, and the Christian Life. *Track's* booklets are theologically rich, yet accessible. They seek to engage and challenge the student without dumbing things down.

One definition of a track reads: *a way that has been formed by someone else's footsteps.* The goal of the *Track* series is to point us to that 'someone else'—Jesus Christ. The One who forged a track to guide His followers. While we cannot follow this track perfectly, by His grace and Spirit He calls us to strive to stay on the path. It is our prayer that this series of books would help guide Christ's Church until He returns.

In His service,

John Perritt
RYM's Director of Resources
Series Editor

Introduction

═══

GOT QUESTIONS?

A Muslim family just moved in next door. They are so religious. They are great neighbors. They speak of Allah and Allah's will all the time. One of their daughters is my age and we've become friends. Does she believe in the same God I do?

How do I know this is all real and true? I grew up in church. I've always had a Bible. I've seen people praying their whole life. Is Christianity true?

I've only been to one funeral, my grandfather's. All they wanted to talk about was that he is in heaven now. How can we know that?

My older brother came home for Christmas from college. He told me about one of his professors who really hates the Bible. He calls it a book that promotes slavery, injustice, and cruelty to women. It is really intolerant of just about everything. I said to my brother, 'what did you say to all that?' He said, 'I didn't really say anything. That prof knew the Bible better than I did and I really didn't have an answer for him.' Are there answers?

I finally got some courage to talk to my friend at school about Christ. I told him that he had to know about Christ and believe in Christ if he wanted to be saved. I thought it was going well, then he said, 'What? I have to believe in your Jesus or I'm the worst person ever and I'm going to hell? What kind of a person are you and what kind of a religion do you believe?' I didn't see that coming. What do I say to him next time I see him?

WHERE ARE THE ANSWERS?

These are all huge questions. Important questions. They are not simply questions about life and death. They are questions about eternal life and eternal death. So where do we find the answer key for these questions?

The short answer is: apologetics. But that raises another question: what is apologetics?

First, apologetics is not saying you are sorry for your faith or your beliefs. That's apologizing. Apologetics means to give a defense, to have an answer. It means to have answers for even these hard questions that you get.

As Christians we need to know what we believe, be able to defend those beliefs, and even be able to contend for those beliefs. We don't need to run away from hard questions.

We can run right into those hard questions because we have answers. Those answers are all found in God and in His revelation—the Bible.

Think about all the voices that tell us what to believe and how we should live. Those voices tell us we are free to make our own identity, free to find our own truth, free to be whoever we want to be.

There's the voice of pluralism, which says all religions are equally valid and true. Pluralism tells us to be tolerant and tells us all beliefs are valid. There's the voice of radical relativism, which holds that all truth statements and moral judgments are relative and changing. Relativism tells just about everybody that they can have their own truth and their own morality. There is a radical hedonism, the love and pursuit of pleasure. Hedonism tells even young kids they are free to choose any path they want that brings them the most personal happiness.

'You be you.' 'Find your own truth.' These voices come at us every minute. But there is one voice that alone is true and alone needs to be heard.

These are strange times, hard times to be a Christian of conviction. But these times are no match for God, the truth of His Word, and the beauty and hope found in the life, death, and resurrection of Jesus. In the chapters that follow we'll look at these three big subjects, God, the Bible, and Jesus Christ. When we see that there are compelling reasons to believe in God, to take the Bible as historically reliable, and come face to face with the unique claims and the unique work of Christ then many, many, questions will be answered. In fact, the ultimate questions will be answered.

It's my hope that you will learn these answers to the questions that you are asked and also questions you yourself may be asking. If you're wrestling with some of these questions, I'm so glad you're reading this. It's also my hope that you will have compassion and confidence. As you think about sharing the gospel and defending the faith, remember that you were once lost. You were once the enemy of God. We have to be wise and we have to be compassionate as we share the gospel with the lost. And we can be confident. Our confidence is not based on how smart we are, or on how persuasive we might be. Our confidence rests solely on God, on the beauty and truth of the Bible, and on the surety of the person and work of Christ.

Let's get started with a word from Peter, Paul, and Mary.

1. Peter, Paul and Mary

A fisherman, a scholar, and a young lady. The Bible is full of interesting people. We can learn something from all of them. As we jump into apologetics, let's start with examples of three apologists from the Bible: Peter, Paul, and Mary. They were also a folk music group in the 1960s—ask your parents (or maybe your grandparents!).

PETER: A CLEAR COMMAND

Peter was an unlikely author of New Testament books. He wasn't a scholar. He was a fisherman, who apparently could swing a sword if needed. In the darkest and most bitter hour of his life, he denied his Savior. Yet, by God's grace, Peter went on to write two epistles (or letters). Right in the middle of his first epistle, Peter writes:

But in your hearts honor Christ the Lord as holy, always being prepared to make a defense to anyone who asks you for a reason for the hope that is in you; yet do it with gentleness and respect (1 Pet. 3:15).

The words 'to make a defense' are also sometimes translated 'to give an answer.' The Greek word here is apologia, from which we get the word apologetics. This word was used in the context of courtrooms. Here's the scene: You're on trial. You've been accused. Now, you have to give an answer, you have to make your defense. Apologetics is giving answers, making a defense for the Christian faith.

Peter uses this word in the verb form of a command. And he is not speaking to pastors or to scholars or to philosophers. He's speaking to everyone. Old, young, men, women. Every Christian is under the obligation of this command. Every Christian is to be an apologist. There's much more we can learn from this one verse, so let's dig in and see the when, the what, the who, and the how of apologetics.

The When: Did you notice when we are to be prepared to give an answer? Always. We are to be always ready to defend the faith. That is quite an expectation. It means we give an answer when we might not feel like it. It means we need to be ready, to be prepared. It means we need to study and know some things.

The What: Peter does not use the word gospel in this passage. Instead, he uses a word that speaks to the effects of the gospel. He says we are to give an answer to anyone who asks 'for the *hope* that is in us.' These Christians were persecuted for their faith. They were marginalized in their culture. Yet, they had hope. That doesn't seem to make sense. How can suffering people have hope? They were living in such a way that the effects of the gospel in their lives were noticed. When we are defending Christianity we are ultimately defending the gospel. The 'what' of apologetics is the gospel. That may very well entail the existence of God, the reliability of the Bible, the understanding of human beings as sinful. But this verse, this command, reminds us that ultimately apologetics is about the gospel.

The Who: (That's another music group, but let's not digress.) Remember, Peter's audience was persecuted. And Peter says give an answer to 'anyone who asks.' Anyone includes everyone. It would include the very people who are persecuting them. This reminds us that no one is beyond the gospel, and that we have an obligation to share the gospel to give an answer to anyone.

The How: Peter ends this verse by telling us that we give an answer with gentleness and respect. That is yet another high expectation. Everyone deserves our respect because everyone is made in the image of God. We're not to be harsh and rough and unkind. One thing that can help us here is to remember that we too were once the enemies of God. Were it not for the work of the Holy Spirit and the grace of God, we would be worthy of nothing but judgment. Being a Christian should give us a hefty dose of humility. We know we do not deserve God's grace. He freely gave it to us. He freely saved us.

The Why: Why do we practice or engage in apologetics? Because people are lost. People are born in darkness and live in darkness. If someone never knows Christ, then that person will live in darkness for all of eternity. Apologetics is not a matter of life and death. It is a matter of eternal life and eternal death. Take a look at 1 Peter 3:18. Peter writes:

For Christ also suffered once for sins, the righteous for the unrighteous, that he might bring us to God, being put to death in the flesh, but made alive in the Spirit.

Here Peter gives us the gospel. We see the work of Christ. He was perfect, holy, righteous, and sinless. He was the spotless lamb who lived in perfect obedience and suffered and died. In His death, He took upon Him the penalty of all our sin and He endured the wrath of God. This is the great exchange. Christ takes our unrighteousness and gives us His righteousness. And because He did that for us, He brings us to the Heavenly Father. Christ brings us to God. Without Christ people will die in their sins and will come under the wrath of God. That is why we, in obedience to this command, practice apologetics.

In 1 Peter 3:15, Peter gives the command for apologetics. In Acts 17, Paul provides an example of apologetics in practice.

PAUL: A COMPELLING EXAMPLE

If you have taken a speech class, or when you do, I have some inside information for you. The number one main thing that you must learn is this: Know your audience. Of course, it's necessary to know your subject. You have to know your stuff. Don't take that 'fake it 'til you make it' approach. That rarely ends well. So it's a given to know that you must know your subject. If you're giving a speech on being a bitcoin trader you'll need more than a Wikipedia article in your arsenal. You have to know your stuff.

You can, however, know everything there is to know about the rise and fall of bitcoins, the metaverse(s), NFTs, and crypto wallets, but what do you know about your audience? How are you going to connect what you know with what they need to know? How are you going to help them? What are their questions?

Let's apply this to apologetics and let's use Paul as an example. In Acts 17 Paul is at Athens, the philosophical capital of the Greco-Roman world. These people loved philosophy. They, after all, gave us Socrates, Plato, and Aristotle. That is to say that Paul is in the philosophical capital of a philosophical world. So, what does he do?

As we break down Acts 17, we see the lead up to the speech in verses 16-21, we have the speech itself in verses 22-31, and we see the response to the speech in verses 32-34. Each of these parts teaches us about the practice of apologetics.

Acts 17:16-21: The Lead Up

Paul's 'spirit was provoked' (Acts 17:16). Paul had a burden for lost people living in darkness. He knew their only hope was the gospel of Christ. Paul teaches us how to see the world. People can appear like they have it all together, like they are okay. In reality, however, they are not okay—they need Christ. Next, he goes to where the people are. He goes to the synagogue. He goes to the marketplace. He engages people in conversation. Next, he observes as he goes. He looks at their culture and he listens to their talk. He takes some time to get to know his audience.

Finally, Paul connects with His audience. When Paul enters the synagogue, he reasons with the Jews from the Old Testament, showing them how Jesus Christ is the long-promised Messiah. When he walks through the marketplace, he reasons with the Greeks from their philosophy and from a classical understanding of theism.

Acts 17:22-31: Paul's Speech

Then, Paul stands up to address the crowd in verses 22-31. What do we learn here? Again, we see Paul connecting with his audience. He mentions the alter to the unknown God that he had seen. He quotes from Greek poets. We see that he uses nature to point to God. He explains how every human being is created by God and accountable to God. He challenges their worldviews and beliefs. He tells them that a day is coming when they will be judged. And he ends his speech by proclaiming Christ, the One who has risen from the dead.

Acts 17:32-34: The Crowd Responds

Then we have the response. Some mocked, some were ambivalent, and some believed. There's a lesson here for us, too. Not everyone responds positively to the good news of the gospel. *But some believed.* Not just at Athens but everywhere Paul went, he preached the gospel and defended the truth claims of Christianity. Sometimes he was heartily received. Sometimes he was beaten and either left for dead or barely escaped. But people believed. We'll talk more about this later in chapter six, but the results of our practicing apologetics and sharing the gospel are not in our hands. The results are in God's hands. We, like Paul, are called to obey the command to always be ready to give an answer for our hope.

MARY: THE HUMBLE EXAMPLE

One more example of a biblical character who was always ready to give an answer was Mary in Luke 1:46-55. This was different from Paul's speech on Mars Hill in Acts 17. We know Elizabeth, her cousin and the mother of John the Baptist, heard Mary's speech. We don't know if there were any others. The text does not say. But let's look at what we find in Mary's speech, known as the Magnificat (from the opening word 'magnifies').

First, however, consider this. Paul was formally trained. Mary was not. Mary was a young lady from, what we can understand, rather humble circumstances in life. We could even say she was 'ordinary,' nothing special in her position or family connections. While Paul had his training and was a noted scholar, Mary was not. What can we learn from a *humble* example?

In response to the angel's pronouncement that she has been chosen to be the mother of Jesus, the promised Messiah, Mary declares with joy who God is and what He does. Read through Luke 1:46-55 and here's what you'll learn about God.

God is ...

> Savior (v. 47).
> Mighty (v. 49).
> Holy (v. 49).
> Merciful (v. 50).
> Judge (vv. 51-52).
> Faithful (vv. 54-55).

Read through the Magnificat and here's what you'll learn about what God does.

> God ...

> Cares for His children (v.48).
> Does great things (v. 49).
> Shows mercy (v.50).
> Protects His children and Punishes His enemies (vv. 51-53).
> Saves His children through the 'Seed,' Jesus Christ (vv. 54-55).

Mary is an apologist. She was faced with a very challenging circumstance, a surprising circumstance to be sure. She could have responded in any number of ways. She actually responded in declaring who God is and what He does with simple beauty. As you read the Magnificat you can feel her joy and her confidence in God. She wants people to know who God is and what He does.

Peter gives the command to practice apologetics. Paul and Mary are but two of many examples in the pages of Scripture of obeying the command. On this biblical foundation let's turn to practicing apologetics today.

MAIN POINT

The Bible commands that we practice apologetics and provides examples of the practice of apologetics.

QUESTIONS FOR REFLECTION

- What do you think of all that Peter includes in his command to practice apologetics in 1 Peter 3:15? How can you begin obeying this command?
- This chapter looks at Paul's example in Acts 17. What can you learn from Paul's example in Acts 14:8-18?
- How is the example of Mary an encouragement to you?

2. Grilled Hot Dogs Need a Hot Dog Griller

It is summertime, school is out, and you are throwing the classic backyard party for your friends. You've got the volleyball net set up. You've got a great playlist. You've got chips and soda. And you have that one last crowning piece to it all: You have grilled hot dogs. Ah, summer.

But here's the thing. Hot dogs don't grill themselves. Grilled hot dogs don't appear out of nowhere. Here is a very philosophical point that we can make about your perfect backyard summertime party:

Grilled hot dogs must have a hot dog griller.

Plato and Aristotle could not be prouder of us for coming to this conclusion. And neither could Paul and Augustine and John Calvin. What we have in this scenario is the classical argument for the existence of God that goes by the name of the cosmological argument for the existence of God. I know many of you have probably never said 'cosmological argument' in your life or talked about this idea with your friends, so hang in there. I'll explain how it fits into everyday life.

The cosmological argument is built on the law of cause and effect, which states that every effect has an equal than or greater cause. Philosophers observed this. In fact, everyone observes this. Grilled hot dog eaters observe this law of cause and effect.

One conclusion we can draw from the law of cause and effect is the impossibility of something coming from nothing. Everything comes from something. This leads us to the most basic observation we can ever make: There is something. That something is the universe, the cosmos. (That's why we call it the cosmological argument.)

In the rest of this chapter, we'll explain the cosmological argument and we'll return to Acts 17 to see how Paul uses that cosmological argument. We'll offer ways you can use this argument to show that belief in God is rational. In fact, belief in God is the only belief that makes sense of the universe and of existence. If you have ever struggled with doubts of God's existence this can be a very helpful argument for you to know that God does indeed exist.

WHEN WE DON'T SEE THE CAUSE

Think back to your summer party. You may have not seen the grill. You may not have seen the hotdogs being grilled. But you were handed a grilled hot dog. We were not there for the beginning of the universe. We do not see God. In fact, the Bible tells us He dwells in inaccessible light. How do we know He exists? We do not start with the cause, rather we start with what we can see and what we can know: the effect.

Writing in the 1200s, Thomas Aquinas said this, 'When an effect is better known to us than the cause, from the effect we proceed to the knowledge of the cause.'[1] Let's unpack that.

We know the world. We see the world, hear it, smell it, touch it, taste it. We live in it and we learn, continually, about it. It is visible and knowable and, as we study it and think about it, the world reveals to us how it works. We know the law of gravity is at work. We know there is order and structure. We begin to sense the

---

1. Thomas Aquinas, *Summa Theologiae, Prima Pars 1-49* (The Aquinas Institute: Lander, Wyoming, 2012) 19.

natural laws that are at work. We see simplicity in the world and we see complexity. We see beauty. We see justice and we see injustice. There is much that can be known about the 'effect,' that is to say there is much that can be known about the world.

The 'effect is better known to us,' as Aquinas says, because we live in the effect and all of our senses are tuned in to it. But the cause is not visible, not apparent to our physical senses.

Consider watching a movie. We watch the movie. We hear the movie. If it's a full experiential theater like at a theme park, the movie might even splash water on us. We feel it. But the moviemakers are hidden and unknown. They become known when we trace the movie back to the movie's creators. Movies don't exist without moviemakers (and the hundreds of names that roll by in the credits). We trace back to the cause from the effect.

R. C. Sproul put it this way, 'The existence of this world's Creator can be surmised through a study of nature as well as from the Bible. In other words, one does not have to read the Bible to know that God exists...The Creator's existence has been exclusively proven through his creation.'[2] Let's return to Acts 17 and see how Paul uses this argument of cause and effect, how Paul uses creation itself, to make a case that the Creator, God, exists.

HE DID NOT LEAVE HIMSELF WITHOUT WITNESS

Paul actually uses the cosmological argument in two places, at Lystra in Acts 14 and at Athens in Acts 17. In Acts 14, Paul healed a man and the crowds started declaring that Paul and Barnabas were the Greco-Roman gods Zeus and Hermes. Paul immediately rushed in to stop them and instead pointed them to the true God. This is what he said to these pagan Romans who likely had never read one verse of the Bible:

Men, why are you doing these things? We are also men of like nature with you and we bring you good news, that you should turn from these vain things to a living God, who made the heaven and the earth and the sea and all that is in them. In past generations he allowed all nations to walk in their own ways. Yet he did not leave himself without witness, for he

---

2.   R. C. Sproul, *Defending Your Faith: An Introduction to Apologetics* (Wheaton: Crossway, 2003) 83.

did good by giving you rains from heaven and fruitful seasons, satisfying your hearts with food and gladness (Acts 14:15-17).

A key phrase in this passage is: *he did not leave himself without a witness.* That witness is the world. This world that gives us food and joy. This good world with all the beauty and variety and wonder of nature is a testimony to God. David declares this in Psalms 8 and 19. Paul says this again in Acts 17.

Men of Athens, I perceive that in every way you are very religious. For as I passed along and observed the objects of your worship, I found also an altar with this inscription: 'To the unknown god.' What therefore you worship as unknown, this I proclaim to you. The God who made the world and everything in it, being Lord of heaven and earth, does not live in temples made by man, nor is he served by human hands, as though he needed anything, since he himself gives to all mankind life and breath and everything. And he made from one man every nation of mankind to live on all the face of the earth, having determined allotted periods and the boundaries of their dwelling place, that they should seek God, and perhaps feel their way toward him and find him. Yet he is actually not far from each one of us, for 'In him we live and move and have our being' as even some of your own poets have said, 'For we are indeed his offspring' (Acts 17:22-28).

As you read through this you begin to see what Paul says about God and what he says about humanity, using two sources: nature and Greek poets. Here's what Paul declares

God...	We...
is Creator of everything	are created
needs nothing (is complete in Himself)	are dependent beings
is Sovereign over His creation	are designed and created for a purpose
will judge in righteousness	will be judged

Paul wants these Athenians to know that God exists. He's the Creator. Therefore, we are created and we are religious beings. Knowing who God is has everything to do with knowing who we are. We start with the fact that we are created. We did not bring ourselves into existence. We are an effect with a cause. The immediate cause is our parents, but if you trace the causal chain back, all the way back, you get to Adam, the first man.

People have raised any number of objections to this argument. We came from evolutionary processes, some would say. This needs to be thought through. If we go all the way back to the big bang, we still have that moment, that split-second before the big bang. What existed then? If nothing existed, then here's what is being said: Everything in the world comes from nothing. But we see that only nothing comes from nothing. A thing, any thing, must have a cause.

Now go back to Acts 17:25 and this phrase: *as though God needed anything.* Paul is saying that God needs nothing. He is a self-existing being. He is what philosophers call a necessary being. All other beings are contingent beings. A contingent being is dependent, needing another being for its existence. A necessary being is independent. What Paul is declaring here is that God, as a necessary being, eternally is. Aristotle spoke of the 'Unmoved Mover' and of the 'Uncaused Cause.' He argued that there must be a being outside the chain of cause and effect, a First Cause. Paul is telling these philosophical heirs of Aristotle that God is that First Cause. God is the Unmoved Mover. But Paul adds that God is also Judge.

We also speak of the *teleological argument* for the existence of God. Telos, like cosmos, is another Greek word and it means order or design or purpose. Not only does the world exist, but it shows intense design and purpose. This points not simply to a cause, but to an intelligent cause, to a designer. This is often referred to as the Intelligent Design argument.

C. S. Lewis, among others, also speaks of the moral argument for God's existence. He makes the point that we all have an innate sense of justice. No parent has ever had to teach a child to say, 'That's not fair.' If we have a sense of justice and laws of morality, then, Lewis reasoned, there must be a Lawgiver. The innate sense of morality and justice that exists universally points to a 'Lawgiver.' Just as the universe traces back to God, so justice leads us to God.

Here's a summary of these three arguments for God's existence:

The Effect	Points to	The Cause
Cosmological Argument		
The *Cosmos* exists.	Therefore,	The First and Necessary Cause exists.
Teleological Argument		
The *Cosmos* reveals Design/ *Telos*.	Therefore,	The Intelligent Designer exists.
Moral Argument		
There is an innate, universal sense of justice.	Therefore,	The Lawgiver exists.

God has not left Himself without a witness. This world, and we His creatures, are a testimony to God. Theologians call this general revelation or natural theology. Then we turn to the pages of the Bible, called special revelation, and we find in the very first verse, Genesis 1:1, the declaration of the name of this Designer, Lawgiver, Perfect Being, and First and Necessary Cause. The name is God. And as we read His revelation we discover more and more of who God is as powerful, eternal, merciful, just, and holy.

Everyone who has ever eaten a grilled hot dog knows that if you have a grilled hot dog you must have a hot dog griller. It is entirely irrational to think that a hot dog came from nothing and proceeded to grill itself. Here's the question to get your non-Christian friends thinking about God. Ask them to explain where the world came from. Ask them to explain the cause of the effect that is this world. The answer cannot be nothing, for only nothing comes from nothing.

There are actually two important points made here in this discussion of God as the cause of all things. The first point concerns the origin of life. God is the source of all that exists. How did we get here? How did I get here? The answer is God created all things. The second point concerns the purpose of life. 'Why am I here? What is the purpose of my life?' The answer is God created us for Himself. God is both the source and purpose of life. Helping people think about that and challenging people to think about that is the first step towards the gospel.

MAIN POINT

God has not left Himself without a witness in this world. As every effect has a cause, the world (the effect) is a witness to the existence of the eternal God (the cause).

QUESTIONS FOR REFLECTION

- In addition to grilled hot dogs and the making of movies, what are some other examples to illustrate the law of cause and effect that might be helpful in getting people to think about the origin of the universe?

- How does the teleological argument for God build on the cosmological argument for God? Make sure you have a good grasp of each one.

- In addition to Acts 14 and 17, what does Psalm 19:1-6 teach about nature's witness and testimony to God?

3. Old Rocks, Ancient Scrolls, and John Ran on Ahead

===

'The Bible is a dangerous book. It hates homosexuals, hates women, and promotes slavery.'

'The Bible is full of lies and contradictions. It can't be trusted.'

'The Bible is no different than any other religious book. It is not unique or the exclusive word on religion.'

These are just a few of the things people say about the Bible. How do we respond? You may not have such hostile questions yourself, but you may be wondering how you can know that the Bible is reliable. This is a crucial question for apologetics and for us as Christians. While we learn about God from the book of nature, we only learn who Christ truly is and what He has done to accomplish our salvation in the Bible. The Bible is our source for the gospel. Additionally, for us as Christians the Bible is the sole authority in our lives. The Bible alone is God's Word full of truth and authority. Let's primarily focus on the apologetic question and demonstrate Scripture's uniqueness and reliability. Along the way, we'll also learn as Christians that we can indeed trust the Bible and know for certain that it is God's Word to us.

Let's be clear on one significant point. We accept the Bible as true because the Bible declares itself to be the authoritative, reliable, and true Word of God. As you read the Bible you trip over this expression, 'Thus says the Lord.' The Bible makes continual reference to its divine origin. What this chapter intends to do is show corroboration and support for that claim. We have reasons why we can believe the Bible is exactly what it claims to be. Let's look at external evidences and support, the internal consistency and nature of the Bible, and a comparison and contrast of the Bible with other religious texts.

OLD ROCKS

One of the most fascinating features of the Bible is that for being a supernatural revelation from God it is very ordinary. The Bible talks about real people who lived in real times.

Sometimes it recounts heroic deeds and miraculous moments, but sometimes it rather plainly describes people, places, and events. The Bible takes place in space and time. We'll see later how that differentiates the Bible from other religious texts, but here's what that means for now. If the Bible recounts events taking place in space and time, then we can look for corroboration of those events.

Here are a few key archaeological discoveries related to the Old Testament. A stela is an ancient upright stone that bears an inscription. The Merneptah Stela was discovered in 1896 and dates to the thirteenth century B.C. and the reign of the Egyptian Pharoah Merneptah. This inscription, recounting the Pharoah's military exploits, contains the earliest external evidence to the nation 'Israel.'

The Moabite Stone may be seen in the Louvre Museum in Paris. Discovered in 1868, it records the deeds of Mesha, the King of Moab in the ninth century B.C. Much of the inscription speaks of his encounters with Israel's King Omri and corroborates events recorded in 1 Kings 16 and 2 Kings 3.

There's also the Black Obelisk of Shalmaneser which may be seen in the British

Museum. It stands six-feet tall and records the accomplishments of the Assyrian King Shalmaneser from the ninth century B.C. It records the paying of tribute to Shalmaneser by Jehu, King of Israel.

Various Babylonian stones and documents record the presence of Israelites in Babylon during their exile. One tablet in particular documents rations given to Jehoiachin and his family, as mentioned in 2 Kings 25:27-30.

And then there is the very small but hugely significant Cyrus Cylinder displayed in the British Museum which measures about the size of your index finger. The cylinder praises Cyrus, the sixth-century B.C. ruler of Persia, for his magnanimous act of allowing conquered peoples to return to their lands and rebuild their cities and temples. This is exactly what is recorded in Isaiah 45 and the books of Ezra and Nehemiah, which tell of Israel's return to the land and undertaking the rebuilding of the city of Jerusalem and of the temple. Ezra and Nehemiah are historical accounts of the event. Isaiah, as a prophecy, speaks of Cyrus by name (44:28 and 45:1) a hundred years before he was even born. What's more, skeptics of the Bible thought that these chapters in Isaiah and the book of Ezra were entirely myth because Cyrus, being the world's worst tyrant up until that time, would never simply release an exiled people and let them go back and rebuild. The Cyrus Cylinder, however, states that this is exactly what happened.

These archeological finds, and more that we have not mentioned, do not prove that the Bible is the Word of God.[1] What they do, however, is support accounts as recorded in the Bible and as such play an important role in supporting the Bible's self-claim that is the authoritative, reliable, and true Word of God. When we as Christians claim that the Bible is the Word of God and is to be trusted, we are not taking a leap into the dark. We are not just hoping that is true. Not only do we have external evidences, but we also have the internal consistency of the Bible.

NO OTHER BOOK LIKE IT

The Bible is the most unique book of all time. (I know, unique does not need the qualifier 'most,' but in this one case it is called for.) The

---

1. For a helpful tool, see *Archaeology Study Bible* (Crossway, 2017). This study Bible has many helpful notes on particular texts, sidebars, and articles detailing archaeological discoveries related to particular biblical accounts.

Bible was written over a span of over twelve-hundred years. It was written by thirty-nine different authors from various walks of life, backgrounds, and education. It was written in three languages on three different continents. And yet, despite all that diversity it is one unified book, telling one unified story, and proclaiming one unified message. There has never been any other book even remotely like the Bible.

The Bible also contains fulfilled prophecy. We already mentioned the specific prophecy of Cyrus a hundred years before his birth. But consider all of the Old Testament prophecies related to the birth of Christ, including that the Messiah would be born in Bethlehem (Micah 5:2). Jesus came into Jerusalem riding a donkey, as prophesied in Zechariah 9:9-10. He was despised, rejected, beaten, and taken as a lamb to the slaughter, all as prophesied in Isaiah 53. There is the prophecy of the flood, of Abraham and his descendants entering the Promised Land, and of both the slavery in and the exodus from Egypt. There is prophecy of Israel's capture and exile, as well as prophecy of Israel's return to Jerusalem.

In addition to the internal consistency and fulfilled prophecy, we also have the Bible's character. It is beautiful literature. It tells tales as fascinating as any of the epic movies playing on our screens. It has poetry that rivals any lines that have been written over the ages. It has brief epistles with clear and compelling arguments. The Bible is a work of art.

And yet the Bible is also ordinary. That sounds like I'm contradicting what I just said about the Bible's high literary character. But consider this. The most epic event in the entire Bible is the death and resurrection of Jesus Christ. The whole Bible has been leading up to this moment. It is the most pivotal moment in all of human history. Yet in the Bible's account of this event, the gospel of John makes a point to mention that John outran Peter as they went to the tomb after hearing from Mary Magdalene that Jesus' tomb was empty. Now John actually never names John as the winner in this footrace—the text refers to 'the other disciple' (John 20:1-4)—yet the Bible includes what may be considered a mundane if not unnecessary detail. Why include it? It is evidence that this event really happened.

These kinds of historical and specific details are all through the Bible. The Bible takes place in real places, real cities, and real countries, and on real seas, lakes, and rivers. The Bible's events play out before real pharaohs, kings and rulers. Herod was a real king. Pontius Pilate was a real person. There is simply too much happening in the Bible to simply write it off as myth and dismiss it as the product of fanciful imaginations. The Bible's historical character demands that we pay attention to it.

Here's the bottom line. The Bible claims to be a divine book. The Bible is unique, and the Bible is corroborated by external evidence. The Bible, however, is not the only religious book that claims to be the Word of God and a definitive and true revelation. How does the Bible compare to other religious texts?

NOTHING COMPARES

Read any other religious text. It is unlike the Bible. Consider the Quran, The Book of Mormon, the Upanishads of Hinduism, or the sayings of Buddha.

The Quran is constructed of Surrahs, or chapters, that are transcriptions of the visions of Muhammad that he claimed to receive, in a trance-like state, directly from Allah. There are many challenges here. Chief among them is how do you corroborate or substantiate this? This entire text rests on the self-claims of one person. To accept the Quran as the revelation of God requires a boatload of trust and a leap of faith.

The Book of Mormon came from Joseph Smith's discovery of gold tablets and the Urim and Thummim from the angel Moroni. He translated this language of ancient unknown characters, what he called 'Reformed Egyptian,' on the tablets by using the Urim and Thummim as seer stones. Scribes recorded his translations of the books that comprise the Book of Mormon. The Book of Mormon has wide chunks of 'historical material' that defies corroboration. In fact, the whole process defies corroboration and a whole religion, Mormonism, is built on trusting the word of one man—Joseph Smith.

The Upanishads of Hinduism and the sayings of the Buddha for Buddhism fall into a similar category. They contain the thoughts of self-proclaimed prophets or seers who reveal the transcendent mysteries of life which they personally have discovered.

Against these religious texts stand the Bible. It too makes self-claims. But a significant difference is that the Bible and the events it records occur in space and time. It lends itself not to blind faith, but to examination. Here's a key example returning again to the pivotal event of the resurrection of Jesus Christ.

In 1 Corinthians 15:3-4, Paul offers a succinct statement of the gospel he preached. Then he notes that Jesus appeared to Peter, the other disciples and to 'more than five hundred brothers at one time.' Then he adds, '*most of whom are still alive*' (1 Cor. 15:6). That's Paul's way of saying there are witnesses who saw this. A lot of witnesses. Go find them and ask them. This event, the resurrection of Jesus Christ, really happened as the Bible has recorded it. It was not revealed in a trance or on golden tablets that no one else has ever seen.

Read other religious texts and you will find that nothing compares to the Bible.

Here's one final text to consider, Luke 1:1-4. As he begins to write his historical account, Luke mentions his awareness of other narratives that are from eyewitnesses—which is crucial to weighing the credibility of their accounts. He then tells us he 'followed all things closely,' intends to write an 'orderly account,' and wants his audience to have 'certainty.' This all points to

Luke's precision and accuracy in providing the historical account of the life, ministry, and cross-work of Jesus Christ in the Gospel of Luke. Luke is a careful historian providing a reliable history. He begins the second volume of his history, The Book of Acts, by noting that 'Jesus presented himself alive to them after his suffering by many proofs' (Acts 1:3). Luke is saying there is eyewitness testimony and proof that what is written here about Christ is in fact true.

The Bible is demonstrably reliable. That means we should read it. It merits our attention. As we read it, what do we find? We find it pointing to one person and proclaiming one message: the person of Christ and the gospel. The whole point of defending the reliability of the Bible is for people to read it. The whole point of reading the Bible is to find Christ.

THE POWER OF GOD

I recently heard the testimony of a doctor who had no real exposure to Christianity. He loved to read and so one day he decided he would read the Bible. He started at Genesis 1:1 and kept reading until he finished. When he read the last verse of Revelation he was overcome with conviction of sin. He prayed for mercy and he prayed for salvation in Christ. From that moment forward he was a committed Christian, telling all his friends about his faith and about Christ.

Nabeel Qureshi was a devout Muslim who believed the New Testament to be full of corruptions. Through the challenge of a friend, he embarked on a journey to disprove the Bible and, consequently, the truth claims of Christianity. Instead, he found the Bible to be true and Christ to be his Savior. He became a Christian and an apologist, dedicating his time to defending and contending for the gospel until he died of cancer at the age of thirty-four.

The Bible is the power of God to change lives. It is not merely a fascinating story. It is the living and abiding Word of God.

Hopefully this chapter provides some helpful points to make to your friends who ask you of the hope that is in you. We need to point people to the Bible. We need to show people the gospel as it is taught in the Bible. As we do, we can have confidence in the Bible. It has stood the test of time. It withstands scrutiny. It demonstrates its historical reliability.

Furthermore, it is important to remember that sometimes apologetics is also for Christians. We need our faith strengthened.

We too can be encouraged by having reasons for our faith. Especially in our moment when so many people attack the Bible, we need to not waver or compromise in our conviction of the Bible as God's authoritative and true Word. There truly is no other book like it.

MAIN POINT

The Bible is unique and reliable, unlike any other book ever written and corroborated by external evidences. As such, the Bible is worthy of our attention.

QUESTIONS FOR REFLECTION

- What role do archaeological discoveries and evidences play in our understanding of the Bible's reliability?
- Can you research other archaeological data that corroborates biblical accounts beyond the examples presented in this chapter?
- What conclusion can we reach about the Bible based on its internal characteristics?
- How does the Bible compare/contrast to other religious texts?

4. The Way, the Truth, and the Life

Years ago my wife and I were on vacation and we met Jack. He was the handyman at the place we were staying. We soon learned that Jack spent his time sailing around the world until he ran out of money. Then he would find a hotel or a resort where he could work as a handyman until he saved up enough money to set sail again. The first day we met, Jack asked me what I did and I told him that I taught at a Bible College. He immediately started peppering me with questions about the Bible and about Christianity. He was at best a skeptic. I did my best to patiently answer his questions.

On our last night I went to Jack's boat and rang the bell attached to the side and requested permission to come aboard. Standing with him on the bow, I handed him a Gospel of John. I said you've had all sorts of questions, but I think there is one question that you need to ask yourself. You need to read this Gospel of John and, as you do, ask yourself this question: Who is Jesus? 'Jack,' I told him, 'that is the most important question you can ask and finding the right answer is the most important thing you can do.'

There are any number of places in John that bring the question of who Jesus is front and center. One of those places is John 14:6. John chapter 13 ends with Jesus telling the disciples that He will be leaving them. This leaves them rather anxious and troubled. We know that's how they're feeling because in John 14:1, Jesus says to them, 'Let not your hearts be troubled.' Jesus proceeds to tell them that He is going to prepare a place for them and adds, 'and you know the way to where I am going' (John 14:4). That prompts a frantic question from Thomas, 'Lord, we do not know where you are going. How can we know the way?' (John 14:5).

Thomas did not fully realize what Jesus was talking about and did not even fully realize what he was asking. Thomas thought he was asking Jesus about a place like the places Jesus and the disciples went, places like Galilee or Jerusalem or the towns dotting the map of Israel. What Jesus was talking about was the way to heaven, the ultimate and final destination. Jesus was talking about the way to the Father and the way to eternal life with the Triune God.

So Jesus declares to him in very plain language:

> *'I am the way, the truth, and the life. No one comes to the Father except through me.'*

If you're familiar with these verses, you may miss how shocking they are. *That is the most radical truth statement ever claimed by any person who walked the earth.* It leaves no room for compromise, no room for options. It is utterly exclusive. It is not one, but three radical absolute truth claims, followed by a claim to absolute exclusivity. This is a heavy little verse.

Before we go any further exploring John 14:6, let's take a step back and look at the person who said it. What can we know about Jesus as an historical figure? Who is Jesus?

THE UNIQUENESS OF JESUS IN HISTORY

There is an abundance of historical references to Jesus of Nazareth. In addition to the written testimony of the Gospels, all dating to the first century, there is also early witness to

Christ by Roman historians. Cornelius Tacitus wrote his *Annals*, chronicling the reigns of the Caesars, from 115–117. In writing of the fire that destroyed Rome under the reign of Nero, Tacitus speaks of the violent persecution of Christians and mentions Christ. He writes:

Therefore, to scotch the rumor [that Nero started the fire], Nero substituted as culprits, and punished with the utmost refinements of cruelty, a class of men, loathed for their vices, whom the crowd styled Christians. Christus, the founder of the name, had undergone the death penalty in the reign of Tiberius, by sentence of the procurator Pontius Pilatus.[1]

Suetonius, another Roman historian, refers to Christ and His followers in his *Lives of the Caesars*, published around 120. There are also references to Christ in the writings of the early church fathers. These include the writings of Clement (80s-90s), Ignatius (100s), Irenaeus (late 100s), and Tertullian (circa 200).

---

1. Tacitus, *Annals* 15.44, in *Tacitus V: Annals Books 13–16*, translated by John Jackson, Loeb Classical Library 322 (Cambridge, MA: Harvard University Press, 1937), 283.

There is also the first-century witness of the empty tomb, the witnesses to the resurrection as pointed out by Luke (Acts 1:3) and Paul (1 Cor. 15:6), in addition to the accounts in the four Gospels. There is the reference to Pontius Pilate and Herod, both historical figures. As we mentioned in the last chapter, the Bible takes place in space and time. This is especially true of the life and ministry of Jesus. These are real cities and towns He visited.

THE UNIQUENESS OF JESUS AND HIS MESSAGE

The first thing we need to notice is that Jesus claims equality with God the Father and the biblical authors present Christ as divine. These deity claims run throughout the Gospel of John. It starts on John 1:1 and pulses through the Gospel. In John 8:58, Christ claimed eternality by saying, 'Before Abraham was, I am.' This is only one of the 'I am' sayings of John. When Jesus said this one, the audience knew immediately who He was claiming to be. As soon as He said it the crowd picked up stones to kill Him for blasphemy (John 8:59). His claims of His own person, as the God-man, are unique. We call this the hypostatic union. Jesus is two natures, truly God and truly man, united in one person.

As C.S. Lewis famously quipped, Christ is either Lord, liar, or lunatic. One thing you cannot say about Christ is that He is merely a good man or a good prophet. He claimed much, much more. So, He was either deceiving people or He was delusional. Or, He was and is who He claimed to be: He is Lord.

Jesus' message was also unique. At one point He tells us to take on His burden or yoke, 'For my yoke is easy and my burden is light' (Matt. 11:30). Jesus is contrasting His way of salvation with the religion of the day that demanded obedience to the law and obedience to a whole burdensome system of works.

So many religions require works. They have lists and lists of what must be done. In some cases, even doing everything perfectly still doesn't guarantee salvation. Jesus offers an entirely different message of salvation. His message is one of mercy for sinners and grace for the repentant.

As we think about what we learn of Jesus from history and from the Bible, we realize that there is no other figure as worthy of our attention. We must consider Him and what He has to say. This leads us back to that weighty but simple series of declarations in John 14:6.

I AM THE WAY

We need to see that each of these claims has the definite article. They have 'the' and not 'a.' Secondly, we need to see that each of these is in the singular:

- way not ways
- truth not truths
- life not lives or options.

Jesus is the way. The way to what?

Tom Douglas is a country songwriter whose first number one hit came in 1994 with the song 'Little Rock,' recorded by Colin Raye. That launched a career of hit songs. But Tom often says that all his songs go back to that guy in Little Rock trying to make his way back, to find his way home, to find redemption.

God made us for Himself. Augustine put it this way, 'You made us for yourself and we are restless until we find our rest in you.' We're like sharks, head turning side-to-side, never stopping till we get that next meal, and the next, and the next. The reason is that we are not at rest. We are not at peace.

While God made us for Himself, we chose disobedience. We chose sin and we lost our home, condemned to wander 'East of Eden.' Jesus is the way back home.

Pluralism, which is the belief that there are many ways to salvation, is very popular today. Actually, it was very popular in the first century Greco-Roman world during the writing of the New Testament. Pluralism teaches that there is not one exclusive way but all religions are valid. Religions just use different words and names to teach the same thing. The problem is that's not true.

The world's religions are not complementary but contradictory. Islam insists that Jesus is not God. Christianity is not Christianity without the belief that Christ is the God-man. Buddhism doesn't even have a concept of salvation. Instead, the idea is liberation not from the material world, but liberation from even the distinction between the material world and immaterial world, or getting past the distinction between being and non-being. Not even a surface treatment of the world's religions shows unity among the claims and beliefs of the world's religions. Pluralism holds that contradictory views are all true. That is illogical.

The law of noncontradiction means a thing cannot be 'A' and 'Non-A' at the same time. The law of contradiction is basic to all meaningful and sensible communication and our understanding of the world. God cannot be the Triune God of the Bible and the Allah of Islam at the same time. Jesus cannot be the God-man and merely a prophet at the same time. Pluralism may seem like a way for people of different religions to all get together. But it simply doesn't work.

Christ offers Himself as the exclusive way to God. To the pluralist, Jesus says, 'I am the way.' To the one who is lost, wandering away from home, Jesus says, 'I am the way.'

I AM THE TRUTH

One saying of today that is as grating as fingernails slowly running across a chalkboard or as annoying as the barking of your neighbor's dog when you're trying to sleep, is 'my truth.' You need to find your truth and I have my truth. This is the conclusion of the worldview known as relativism.

There was a time when there was an actual conception of truth. Truth was objective (independent of the subject/not subjective) and absolute (not relative). Objective and absolute truth was exchanged for the idea of only having 'truths' for certain contexts and communities. The emergence of 'my truth' and 'your truth' has now entered the Twilight Zone of absurdity, as if there are as many universes as individual people.

When I fly, I'm always thankful that the plane's pilot does not have his truth. I very much appreciate the idea that he follows the truths of gravity, physics and aerodynamics as he takes off, flies, and lands. It is detrimental to life if we were to push this notion of 'my truth' to its conclusion. It is detrimental to eternal life as well.

Jesus said He was the Son of God. That was His testimony. Then He performed miracles, as recorded in the Bible, that was the evidence of His testimony. Jesus said He was the Messiah. Then He showed from the Old Testament that He was the Messiah, again offering evidence for His testimony. The final evidence for who Jesus said He was and for the work He accomplished is the empty tomb, the resurrection, and the post-resurrection appearances. That is the ultimate evidence for His testimony. Jesus did not make 'bald' claims without anything supporting them.

When Jesus said He is the truth, He was also speaking to the cynical and skeptical. It's easy to be cynical after a generation or two of living in the advertising age. We've all seen the burger on the billboard and the burger that gets handed to us at the drive-thru window. One does not look like the other. Many young people today are cynical. They've seen bad people misuse and abuse religion and religious positions. They don't trust institutions. They know they're not going to get a carefully, perfectly constructed burger. But there stands Christ, saying to the cynic and to the skeptic, 'I am the truth.'

I AM THE LIFE

There has always been a sense of teenage angst. But given the events of the last several years with a global pandemic and subsequent lockdowns, social upheaval, and economic turmoil, there is for many an intensified sense of desperation and anxiety. Your friends, and perhaps even you, feel desperate and hopeless. Some show this by turning to New Age ritual practices, desperate political activism, or simply just posting dark-humored memes on Instagram. Some simply close up in themselves and shut out their family and friends.

There is a philosophical view behind this called Nihilism, the belief in nothing. It is also reflected in the post-World War II philosophy of existentialism, captured in the writings of Jean Paul Sartre and Albert Camus. Nihilist and existentialist ideas haunt movies, pop-culture, pop-music.

The author of Ecclesiastes would agree with some of the ideas here. He says, 'Vanity of vanities, all is vanity.' That is, life apart from God is meaningless and nothingness. Nihilism and existentialism and their cultural manifestations may be right in acknowledging the pain and absurdity in the world, but they are wrong to stop there. They are wrong to say the end of the world, indeed the end of life, is simply a sign that shouts 'Dead End.'

John has two powerful images running through his Gospel and epistles. The image of light over darkness and the image of life over death.

Jesus brings a message of life amidst death, light amidst darkness, hope amidst despair. We live in an age of abundance. Common people today live better than kings of the past. Yet, the world is full of despair. It is because we are not looking to the right place. Or to the right person. As you study the Gospels you see Jesus again and again healing the sick, restoring sight to the blind, caring for those in need. He brought hope to hopeless people. He was a physician for the sick. He came to bring lost people home.

Jesus is the answer to the pluralist, the skeptic, the cynic, the hopeless and the desperate. And that is because He alone is the way to God the Father. Knowing God and being at peace with God is the answer to all of these flawed worldviews. That is all packed in John 14:6. In the next chapter we'll take a deeper look at the gospel and this central message of the Bible.

MAIN POINT

Jesus is unique in all of human history in both the claims He made of His own person and of His work.

QUESTIONS FOR REFLECTION

- Can you think of other biblical texts beyond those mentioned in this chapter that teach the two natures of the true humanity and true deity of Christ?

- How important is getting the person of Christ right (what Jesus is) in order to get the work of Christ right (what Jesus did)?
- Can you think of friends you know that fit the category/categories of pluralism, skepticism, or despair/hopelessness? How might you share John 14:6 with them?

5. Put It All Together

Imagine studying for hours and hours for an exam. You have poured every ounce of your brain into it and you are ready. You show up at the appointed time and place to take the exam. Your teacher puts it in front of you. And you freeze. You look at the exam and you realize you spent all that time studying for the wrong test. Oh, the pain.

That, however, doesn't even begin to illustrate the problem many people have. They go through life pursuing all sorts of things. They ask all sorts of questions and seek answers from all kinds of places. They devote tons of energy to pursuing all sorts of things. And, yet, despite all those efforts they have studied for the wrong exam.

No matter what we pursue or what questions we ask, the ultimate pursuit and the ultimate question is this:

How can I be right with God?

You can get everything else in life right. But if you miss this, you miss everything.

This question gets to the heart of the gospel. So far we have looked at belief in the existence of God, the reliability and uniqueness of Scripture, and the case for the unique claims of the historical figure of Jesus Christ. Now, let's look at the gospel.

FROM WRATH TO PEACE?

The question how can I be right with God entails a very important point: *I am not right with God.* I am wrong with God. Paul's epistle to the Romans offers the fullest discussion of the gospel in the Bible. After the introduction and the statement of the theme in Romans 1:16-17, Paul turns to the need for the gospel. In Romans 1:18 Paul says, 'The wrath of God is revealed …' Think about that. The first word that describes our relationship with God is wrath. Paul adds in Ephesians 2:3 that we are 'by nature children of wrath.' As children of wrath, we are enemies of God.

That's Romans chapter 1. When we get to the opening words of Romans chapter 5, Paul joyfully declares that 'we have peace with God.'

Those are perhaps the most beautiful words you could ever hear or read. We have peace with the almighty, eternal, holy God. How do we move from being under the wrath of God to being at peace with God? The answer comes in Romans chapter 3. God's wrath is revealed against us because we are sinners. We are unrighteous. Paul strings together a whole series of Old Testament quotations in Romans 3:10-18 which vividly depict our predicament.

In Romans 1–3, and in many other biblical passages, we are taught that not only are we sinners, but we are born sinners. We sin because we are sinners. The Reformer Martin Luther realized we are sinners at the root. He used the Latin word radix. That word looks like radical, which is in one way how we should understand what Luther meant. We are radical sinners. But Luther meant something a bit more. The Latin word radix is close to the English word radish. A radish is a root vegetable, because you are eating the root when you eat one. Luther wanted us to understand that we are sinners at the very core of our being. A lot of people do not believe this.

Ligonier Ministries and LifeWay research team up to offer The State of Theology survey every two years.[1] The survey consists of a number of statements on key theological issues and survey participants are asked if they agree or disagree with the statements One of the statements for the 2022 survey was:

Everyone is born innocent in the eyes of God.

When put to a general American audience 71 per cent agreed. That means that seven out of every ten Americans do not believe we are born sinners. When put to evangelicals, 65 per cent agreed. The survey also reveals that people have difficulty grasping the full weight of sin. Another statement reads:

Even the smallest sin deserves eternal damnation.

How do Americans and evangelicals in particular fare on this? 69 per cent of Americans agreed and 40 per cent of evangelicals agreed. We have difficulty seeing ourselves as sinners because we really don't know who God is. He is holy. Righteous. Pure. So, it is true. Even the smallest sin is worthy of damnation.

---

1.   Visit Stateoftheology.com for the full survey results.

GUILT AND SHAME

One very crucial way this lack of taking the weight of sin seriously manifests itself regards guilt and shame. When Adam and Eve sinned, they immediately covered themselves. That is shame. Shame is subjective. Some people blush at anything, while some people keep that poker face on. Guilt, on the other hand, is both an objective state and a subjective feeling.

Some schools of psychology, chief among them B. F. Skinner and behaviorism, taught that we have nothing to be ashamed of because we are guilty of nothing. There are simply behaviors. There is nothing we ought to do. There are only things that we do.

The reality is, however, that we are all guilty before God. If you go to the end of Romans chapter 1 you see a dynamic at work where total depravity, that is our radical sinfulness, is a downward trending cycle. The more we sin, the more we are given over to sin and the more 'acceptable' even heinous behaviors become. Eventually, shame disappears from the culture. But guilt never goes away.

Because our relationship with God is disrupted, we are not at peace with one another in our sinful state. As one philosopher put it, we are in a war of all against all. We are also not at peace with our own selves. That is what intense guilt is like. Guilt is a war within our very selves.

WAY OUT

Guilt is a real problem. Sin is a real predicament. I love traveling the underground subway in London, the 'Tube.' At every stop, as you step off the car onto the platform you see a sign and you hear a voice that says, 'Mind the gap.' The 'gap' is the small space between the end of the subway car and the platform. It's easy to cross, but if you're not paying attention you could trip on the gap. The gap between a holy God and a sinner is no small space. It can't be stepped over. In fact, it's not a gap. It's a chasm—and we can't cross it.

There's another sign that you see all over those London Tube stations. It's an arrow with the words 'Way Out.' There is one way out of our predicament as sinners. There is only one way to cross the chasm that separates us as sinners from God. That way out is Christ. We cannot mind the gap. But Christ did.

Let's go back to Romans 3. In verse 21, Paul makes an abrupt turn with the little word, 'but,' and then follows with some of the most beautiful words in all of Scripture:

> *But now the righteousness of God has been manifested apart from the law, although the Law and the Prophets bear witness to it—the righteousness of God through faith in Jesus Christ for all who believe. For there is no distinction: for all have sinned and fall short of the glory of God, and are justified by his grace as a gift, through the redemption that is Christ Jesus (Rom. 3:21-24).*

The gospel literally means 'good news.' And the good news is that we can have peace with God. We can be pulled out from under His wrath. The only way that can happen is because of what Christ did and by faith in Christ and in Christ alone.

We need to read on to Romans 3:25, where Paul says of Christ:

> *Whom God put forward as a propitiation by his blood, to be received by faith.*

The word propitiation means to satisfy an offended deity by blood sacrifice. We see this in a shadow form in Genesis 3. When Adam and Eve sinned and after they were confronted by God, 'God made for Adam and for his wife garments of skins and clothed them' (Gen. 3:21). The final plague in Egypt was the taking of the firstborn son of every family. To escape you had to slay a lamb and cover the doorposts of your house with its blood. Then, once the tabernacle and later the temple were established, we have the sacrificial laws and especially the Day of Atonement (Lev. 16:15-34; 23:26-32).

As we move to the New Testament, we see John the Baptist say of Jesus right as Jesus began His public ministry, 'Behold, the Lamb of God, who takes away the sin of the world' (John 1:29). Christ, the Lamb of God, both lived and died for us. He was what theologians call actively and passively obedient. He both kept the law, which is active obedience, and paid the penalty for our breaking of the law, which is passive obedience. His resurrection is God's acceptance of Christ's sacrifice on our behalf (Heb. 2:17; 7:25; 9:11-28;10:11-16).

R. C. Sproul had a way of making theology clear and simple. He often did this by saying the gospel is as simple as these three points.

1. God is holy.
2. I am a sinner.
3. Christ is my only substitute.

ALONE

The key to understanding the gospel is the Word alone. Salvation is by grace alone, through faith alone, in Christ—the sacrificial Lamb—alone. These are three of the so-called Five Solas of the Reformation. The Five Solas are:

Sola Scriptura	Scripture Alone
Sola Fide	Faith Alone
Sola Gratia	Grace Alone
Solus Christi	Christ Alone
Soli Deo Gloria	The Glory of God Alone

Salvation is not by faith plus works. It is not by Christ's work plus our efforts. If we remember that God is holy and we are sinners then it will always be sola: faith alone, grace alone, Christ alone. There is no room for boasting in ourselves. Salvation as the work of God alone is for the glory of God alone.

We remember from Ephesians 2:8-9 that faith is a gift administered by the Holy Spirit. There is nothing we do to get saved. There is nothing we can do. In fact, faith in Christ is realizing that Christ alone is my Savior and all I need to do, what I have to do, is trust in Him for my salvation. In the words of the Heidelberg Catechism Q&A #60, 'All I need to do is to accept this gift of God with a believing heart.' We can say, 'Have mercy on me, a sinner,' and we can know that Christ is mighty to save. What a wonderful gift our salvation is. What a beautiful thing it is to say that I am forgiven, I am no longer guilty, and I stand at peace with God.

When we talk about Christ removing the penalty of sin for us, we are also talking about Christ removing our shame and guilt. This is how we can be at peace with God, at peace with one another, and even at peace within our own soul. In the hymn 'Rock of Ages,' we sing of Christ as the 'double cure.' When Christ died and rose again, He saved us from the guilt and power of sin. We are no longer guilty before God and sin no longer has power over us.

IN CHRIST

Spend time reading Romans 5. As Paul closes that chapter, he contrasts what it means to be 'In Adam,' versus being 'In Christ.' The chart below summarizes Romans 5 and other biblical teaching to begin to plumb the depths of our great and wonderful salvation. This also becomes a helpful way to talk about the gospel. Helping people see who they are, in an ultimate sense, in Adam. Then, in turn, helping them see what Christ has truly done for those who trust in Him for salvation.

In Adam	In Christ
Unrighteous	Righteous
Condemned	Justified
Dead	Alive
Guilty	Forgiven
Slave	Free
Self-Centered	God-Centered
Alienated	Reconciled
Child of Wrath	Peace with God

Remember Peter's command for apologetics in 1 Peter 3:15. We are to always be ready to give an answer for our hope. In John 15:11, Christ tells the disciples, 'I have told you these things that your joy may be full.' In John 10:10, Christ said, 'I have come that they might have life and have it abundantly.'

That's the gospel. Hope. Joy. Life to the full. It's all because in Christ we are redeemed and we are at peace with God. The gospel is the most beautiful message of all time and we have the privilege of sharing it. The kindest thing we could possibly do is not tell people they are okay, or not tell people that they can believe whatever works for them. The kindest thing we can do is tell them that God is holy, we are sinners, and Christ is the only substitute.

MAIN POINT

The gospel is knowing and believing that God is holy, I am a sinner, and Jesus is my only substitute.

QUESTIONS FOR REFLECTION

- Why is it important to start with the holiness of God when we think and talk about the gospel?
- What does it mean that salvation is by grace alone through faith alone in Christ alone? Why is the alone crucial?
- Reflect on the chart of being in Adam as a sinner and in Christ as saved. What does that mean for you in your Christian life? How might you use that in apologetics or evangelism?

6. The Apologist and the Work of God

===

Apologetics is rational. Apologetics is also relational. We've been talking about apologetics. Now, let's talk about the apologist. Let's discuss three things every apologist needs: confidence, courage and conviction, and compassion. And, like saving the dessert for last, let's end this chapter talking about God's role in bringing people to saving faith.

CONFIDENCE

I can remember it like it just happened. I would stretch for the wall while doing laps at swim practice and my coach would gently tap me with a kickboard. (It was the early '80s and coaches could do that.) I'd pull back my goggles, wipe the remaining water from my eyes and look up for his words of wisdom. 'You lack confidence,' he would say and move on. He was right. I would practice and practice and practice. Eventually, I gained confidence. We can gain confidence as we practice apologetics. We can gain confidence as we talk more and more to people about God, Christ, and the gospel. But that is not what I'm talking about here. Our confidence is not in ourselves or in our skills.

Our confidence is in God, in Christ, and in the gospel.

In Psalm 27, David is facing enemies and challenges. Yet, he has a fixation on God who towers over his enemies and challenges. David proclaims:

The LORD is my light and my salvation; whom shall I fear?
The LORD is the stronghold of my life; of whom shall I be afraid?
When evildoers assail me to eat up my flesh, my adversaries and foes, it is they who stumble and fall.
Though an army encamp against me, my heart shall not fear;
though war arise against me, yet I will be confident (Ps. 27:1-3).

God had demonstrated His steadfast love, faithfulness, and power in David's life, time after time. We can easily be timid. They say that public speaking is feared sometimes even more than death. Speaking about ultimate truths to potentially hostile people can be downright terrifying. We can tell ourselves we won't know the right answers, we'll say all the wrong things. In those times, we need to remember that our confidence is in God.

Our confidence is also in Christ. Paul offers us a fascinating autobiographical moment in 2 Corinthians 12. He speaks of a mysterious thorn in his flesh and his efforts to get rid of it. He resolves the matter by realizing that in his own weakness the power of God and of Christ manifests itself. This is the lesson Paul learned:

My grace is sufficient for you, for my power is made perfect in weakness. Therefore, I will boast all the more gladly of my weakness, so that the power of Christ may rest upon me. For the sake of Christ, then, I am content with weaknesses, insults, hardships, persecutions and calamities. For when I am weak, then I am strong (2 Cor. 12:9-10).

Finally, our confidence is not in our words or eloquence. Our confidence is in the gospel, the message we proclaim. When Paul wrote Philippians he was in his first Roman imprisonment. He begins the epistle by speaking of the gospel being known among the Praetorian Guard, the elite forces of the Roman Army that served as protective details (Phil. 1:13). As Paul closes Philippians, he speaks of the gospel making its way into 'Caesar's household' (Phil. 4:22). That Caesar was Nero, the despicable, wicked, tyrant Nero. If the gospel can penetrate into these dark and difficult places, then we can have confidence in the power of the Gospel. God promises that His Word will not return void (Isa. 55:11). The Word of God is powerful and effective.

Confidence in God, Christ, and the gospel leads to courage.

COURAGE AND CONVICTION

Remember the lion from *The Wizard of Oz*? The poor creature lacks courage so much he even scares himself. At one point he goes screaming down a hallway and jumps out of a window! Fear keeps us from sharing the gospel. We fear we'll say the wrong thing. We might fear we'll be rejected. We might fear we'll 'mess it up,' and decide it would be better if someone else shared the gospel.

These fears all make sense, if apologetics is about us. But it is not. It is about God and His Word, Christ and His work, and the gospel and its power. That gives us courage. Church history is full of stories of courage. The early martyrs exhibited courage. Polycarp, deep into his eighties, stood courageously before the Roman Empire in the arena as he gave his life for his Savior. Athanasius stood boldly in the face of false teaching. His motto was, Athanasius *contra mundum,* that is, against the world. Luther stood boldly before the Castle Church doors in Wittenberg and before the Diet of Worms. These were not Super Hero moments like in a Marvel movie. These were people who had a *derived* courage. That is to say, it was a courage that came from knowing that by standing for God, God was standing for them. The courage came from an outside source.

We can be bold; we need to be bold. Not stupid or arrogant. We do not swagger. It all traces back to Psalm 27. No matter what we face as Christians, we can say, 'Yet will I be confident.' We can have courage.

Courage helps us to stand for our convictions in the face of challenges and compromise. We live in a moment of hostility toward Christian beliefs, the Bible, God, and Christ. Too many have cowered in the face of cultural pressure.

They lacked confidence, like me and swimming, and they lack courage, like the lion from *The Wizard of Oz*. We can have confidence in the truth of the gospel and we can have confidence in the God of the gospel.

There's one more thing we need to consider about us besides confidence, courage, and conviction—compassion.

COMPASSION

There is a fascinating little phrase in the middle of Jesus' interaction with the rich young ruler in Mark 10:21. As Jesus interacts with this man, Mark tells us that Jesus 'loved him.' In Luke 19:41, we find Jesus weeping over the lost in the city of Jerusalem. Earlier in Luke 7, He has compassion for a widow who just lost her son. In Matthew 9:36, He had compassion for the crowds, who were 'helpless, like sheep without a shepherd.'

Read through the gospels and you will see with great clarity the example of Christ having compassion. We, too, need compassion for the lost.

We can cultivate compassion by looking to the example of Christ. We can also cultivate compassion by remembering that we were once lost. We were once the enemies of God.

When we speak of God's election, we use the word 'unconditional.' That means that we have no condition in us that causes God to save us. God in His sovereignty freely bestows His grace and calls us to be His sons and daughters. We see this in the election of Israel in Deuteronomy chapters 7 and 10. There was nothing great about Israel. In fact, it was the least of the nations. It was the good pleasure and will of God to love Israel (Deut. 7:5-11).

Martin Luther is likely best known for nailing his Ninety-Five Theses to the church door at Wittenberg on October 31, 1517. Two years later he wrote another set of these for a disputation at Heidelberg. In the final theological thesis, number 28, Luther declares:

The love of God does not find, but creates, that which is pleasing to it.[1]

God did not love us because we had something to offer Him. We had nothing to offer but our sin and rebellion. Yet, He loved us. Yet, He chose us. Yet, He saved us. As we remember this, we can cultivate compassion for the lost.

---

1. Martin Luther, 'Heidelberg Disputation,' in *The Annotated Luther: Vol. 1, The Roots of Reform*, edited by Timothy J. Wengert (Minneapolis: Fortress Press, 2015) 104.

In fact, as we remember this, we can cultivate a great desire to practice apologetics. God's election of us should fill us with humility and gratitude and an overwhelming desire to make God and His gospel known to others.

This leads us to the final, but the most important piece of the puzzle. We have been talking about apologetics as rational and as relational. We have been talking about what the apologist does and who the apologist is. Now, we need to look at the work of God in apologetics and evangelism.

THE WORK OF GOD: CALLING

We begin with the subject we just mentioned, the doctrine of election. In John 6:44, Jesus says, 'No one can come to me unless the Father who sent me draws him.' In Ephesians 1:4, Paul tells us that God 'chose us in [Christ] before the foundation of the world.' And in Romans 8:29-30 we have this glorious unbroken chain of God's election:

For those whom he foreknew he also pre-destined to be conformed to the image of his Son, in order that he might be the firstborn among many brothers. And those whom he predestined he also called, and those whom

*he called he also justified, and those whom he
justified he also glorified.*

Salvation begins with God's sovereign election
and calling. Theologians call it the 'effectual
call.' That means when God calls, those that
are His come. See how Jesus speaks of this as
a shepherd calling his sheep in John 10:27-28.

THE WORK OF THE HOLY SPIRIT: CONVICTING AND REGENERATING

In John 16:8, we learn that the Holy Spirit
convicts of sin. That's important to notice. We
would not know, truly, of our sin and even of
our need for a savior apart from the work of the
Holy Spirit. People numb themselves to their
true condition.

How do they numb themselves? They
pursue pleasure. They seek entertainment.
The word 'amusement,' literally means without
thinking. They pursue self-improvement. They
pursue doing good works. In God's grace, the
Holy Spirit breaks through all those barriers
and lays bare the true human condition.

The Spirit convicts and also regenerates.
This goes back to John 3 and Nick at Night,
or Nicodemus coming to Jesus by the cover of
night. Jesus told this teacher of the Law that he

had to be born again, or born of the Spirit, in order to enter the kingdom of God. We see this doctrine also explained by Paul in Titus 3:4-6. The regenerating work of the Holy Spirit is a washing, a renewal. We are dead in sin and dead people can't do anything. So, the Holy Spirit brings us to life, regenerates us, and we put our faith in Christ and accept Him as our Savior.

THE WORK OF CHRIST: THE CROSS

God the Father calls us to salvation. God the Son accomplished the work of salvation. God the Holy Spirit applies the work of salvation. The key word related to Christ's work comes from Him as He hung on the cross: 'It is finished' (John 19:30). If it is a finished work, then there is nothing that we need to add to it or could add to it. All this is to say that salvation is a work of God.

That is the most comforting and encouraging thing for an apologist to hear. Our job is not to convict or convert. Our job is not to save. Salvation is a divine and supernatural work and can only be accomplished and applied by the Triune God. Our role is to pray and to proclaim. Paul does ask in Romans 10:14, 'How are they to hear without someone preaching?' God has ordained that human beings are the instruments of preaching the gospel. As clay jars, we carry the treasure of the gospel. It is not our calling to save; that work belongs to God.

There is a great mystery here. But there is a great comfort and encouragement here. We are called to be faithful in proclaiming the gospel and we leave the results in God's hands. Remember the response of the crowd to Paul's apologetic speech in Acts 17? Not all believed. That did not mean Paul failed. It means that we trust in the good and wise and perfect will of God. God will accomplish His purposes. We are called to be faithful and may we do so with confidence, courage, and compassion.

MAIN POINT

The apologist can have confidence, courage, and compassion, knowing that salvation, from start to finish, is the work of the Triune God.

QUESTIONS FOR REFLECTION

- Do you feel timid in practicing apologetics or sharing the gospel? How does thinking about our confidence in God, Christ, and the gospel help?
- How can you personally cultivate compassion for the lost? Is there someone

in particular you can pray for and show compassion?

- How does knowing what is the work of the Triune God in calling, convicting and saving help clarify your role in apologetics and evangelism?

Conclusion

Here's one final biblical passage to consider: 2 Corinthians 5:11-21. Corinth was a wicked city. The pursuit of sensual pleasure overran this Roman city. False worldviews clamored in its streets. Yet, in this city there was a church. There were Christians called to live in obedience. They were called, as every Christian is, to be apologists.

In this passage, you see Paul's heart for the lost. You see his urgency to proclaim the gospel. He uses the words 'persuade' and 'implore.' He gives a clear and succinct teaching of the gospel. He lays out for us all that we have in Christ, which compels him to want to share the gospel. He calls us ambassadors, the representatives who bear the message of their King. He appeals to Christ for there is no hope without the gospel. In the middle of this passage, Paul says, 'For the love of Christ controls us.'

May that be true of us. May the love of Christ control us as we live for, defend, and contend for the faith.

Appendix A: What Now?

Often after reading a book like this, it can be easy to go back to living our lives like normal—but we are called to respond and share the gospel. Here are a few ideas of next steps you can take in becoming more confident in sharing the gospel with those around you:

- What is the gospel? Can you think of five biblical texts that clearly set forth the gospel? Can you summarize the gospel in a way that is clear and concise and also biblically accurate? Here are two to consider: 2 Corinthians 5:21 and 2 Corinthians 8:9.
- Make a prayer list of ten or so friends, neighbors, or people you regularly connect with who, as far as you know, are not Christians. Pray for their salvation and pray that God would give you opportunities to share the gospel with them.
- Look up archaeological discoveries related to biblical events, such as the Cyrus Cylinder.

Learn what you can about how these discoveries can corroborate the biblical text.

- Take the Gospel of John challenge. Think of one person that you want to have some conversations with about the gospel. After a few conversations offer them a Gospel of John. Encourage them to ask this as they read it: Who is Jesus, and what is your response? Be ready to follow up with them and answer their questions.
- If you know someone of another religion, read up on that religion and think about the contrast of that religion's view with the Christian view of God, Christ, and salvation. Are you 'always ready' to give an answer for your Christian beliefs if you were to have a conversation with that person?
- Find an older Christian that has a testimony of faithfulness. Ask them how they learned to have compassion for the lost. Be sure to make note of key points from their advice and review those points from time to time.

Do a study of Acts 17:16-34. Remember there are three elements to this passage:

1. The lead up to the speech (17:16-21)
2. Paul's speech (17:22-31)
3. The crowd's response (17:32-34)

What can you learn from each of these as you study Paul's example of practicing apologetics?

Appendix B: Other Books on this Topic

Sinclair Ferguson, *The Heart of the Gospel: God's Son Given for You* (P&R, 2015).

Daniel Hames and Michael Reeves, *What Fuels the Mission of the Church?* (Crossway, 2022).

Sharon James, *Lies We Are Told, the Truth We Must Hold: Worldviews and Their Consequences* (Christian Focus, 2022).

Walt Mueller, A *Student's Guide to Navigating Culture* (Christian Focus, 2021).

Stephen Nichols, *Welcome to the Story: Reading, Living, and Loving God's Word* (Crossway, 2011).

R. C. Sproul, *Defending Your Faith: An Introduction to Apologetics* (Crossway, 2003).

-----, *Making a Difference: Impacting Culture and Society as a Christian* (Baker, 2019).

Appendix C: Key Biblical Passages for Apologetics

How can God be known?
Psalm 8; 19
John 1:1-16
Acts 14:8-19; 17:16-34
Romans 1:18-32
Hebrews 1:1-4

Can I trust the Bible?
Psalm 19:7-14; 119:89-105
Matthew 4:4; 5:17-18
2 Timothy 3:14-17
1 Peter 1:23-25
2 Peter 1:16-21

Who is Christ?
Isaiah 9:6-7; 53
John 8:56-59; 10:17-18; 20:24-31
Colossians 1:15-20; 2:8-20
Hebrews 4:14-16
Revelation 5

What is the gospel?

Genesis 3:15
Romans 3:21-25; 5:12-21
1 Corinthians 15:3-4
Ephesians 2:1-10
1 John 1:9-10; 5:1-12

Reformed Youth Ministries (RYM) exists to serve the Church in reaching and equipping youth for Christ. Passing on the faith to the next generation has been RYM's mission since it began. In 1972, three youth workers who shared a passion for biblical teaching to high school students surveyed the landscape of youth ministry conferences. What they found was a primary emphasis on fun and games, not God's Word. They launched a conference that focused on the preaching and teaching of God's Word – RYM. Over the last five decades RYM has grown from a single summer conference into three areas of ministry: conferences, training, and resources.

- **Conferences:** RYM hosts multiple summer conferences for local church groups in a variety of locations across the United States. Conferences are for either middle school or high school students and their leaders.
- **Training:** RYM launched an annual Youth Leader Training (YLT) event in 2008. YLT is

for anyone serving with youth in the local church. YLT has grown steadily through the years and is now offered in multiple locations. RYM also offers a Church Internship Program in partnering local churches, youth leader coaching and youth ministry consulting services.

- **Resources:** RYM offers a growing array of resources for leaders, parents, and students. Several BIble studies are available as free downloads (new titles regularly added). RYM hosts multiple podcasts available on numerous platforms: The Local Youth Worker, Parenting Today, and The RYM Student Podcast. To access free downloads, for podcast information, and access to many additional ministry tools visit us on the web – rym.org.

RYM is a 501(c)(3) non-profit organization. Our mission is made possible through the generous support of individuals, churches, foundations and businesses that share our mission to serve the Church in reaching and equipping youth for Christ. If you would like to partner with RYM in reaching and equipping the next generation for Christ please visit rym.org/donate.

Christian Focus Publications

Our mission statement —

STAYING FAITHFUL
In dependence upon God we seek to impact the world
through literature faithful to His infallible Word, the Bible.
Our aim is to ensure that the Lord Jesus Christ is presented as
the only hope to obtain forgiveness of sin, live a useful life and
look forward to heaven with Him.

Our books are published in four imprints:

CHRISTIAN
FOCUS

Popular works including biographies, commentaries, basic doctrine
and Christian living.

CHRISTIAN
HERITAGE

Books representing some of the
best material from the rich heritage
of the church.

MENTOR

Books written at a level suitable
for Bible College and seminary
students, pastors, and other serious
readers. The imprint includes
commentaries, doctrinal studies,
examination of current issues and
church history.

CF4•K

Children's books for quality Bible
teaching and for all age groups: Sunday
school curriculum, puzzle and activity
books; personal and family devotional
titles, biographies and inspirational stories — because you are never too young
to know Jesus!

Christian Focus Publications Ltd,
Geanies House, Fearn, Ross-shire,
IV20 1TW, Scotland, United Kingdom.
www.christianfocus.com
blog.christianfocus.com